1

The First Peoples of Tasmania are called palawa. Their language is palawa kani. Tasmania is called lutruwita in palawa kani.

My friend James moved to Hobart for work. The First Nations word for Hobart is nipaluna. Dylan and I decided to visit James. We planned a surfing adventure!

Knowledge Books and Software

I'm Mark - a Wiradjuri and European man from Northern NSW. It takes about three hours to fly to Hobart from my home. You can see the photo of the purinina/Tasmanian Devil, at the airport. These mammals come out at night and are hard to spot. They are meat-eaters. They eat the dead meat of other small animals. They are endangered and protected.

4

5

James, Dylan and I planned to explore lutruwita for a week in a camper van. We packed our food, water, clothes, wetsuits, and surfboards. We said goodbye to James' family and drove to Roaring Beach at tukana/Tasman Peninsula on Day 1. The wind is strong here and roars across the beach. We surfed some great waves!

Knowledge Books and Software

7

Day 2 was my birthday! We grabbed our boards and followed a track to Remarkable Cave. We paddled through the dark cave to a beach on the other side. We were the only ones there. After a big surf, we headed back to our campsite for a yummy dinner. A family of wallabies and possums came to say hello.

Knowledge Books and Software

Long ago, First Peoples made clothes from the skins of possums, kangaroos, and wallabies. They were called cloaks. They were very warm and strong. They were also waterproof. The cloaks grew bigger each year as more skins were added.

Knowledge Books and Software

We woke up to lots of rain on Day 3 and drove to the East Coast. Along the way, we stopped at a lookout and found some wild blackberry bushes. They were very sweet. The rain had cleared by the time we arrived at Binalong Bay. Time for another surf! That night, we used the hot coals from our campfire to cook some yummy spuds.

Knowledge Books and Software

On Day 4, we drove to a beach with big waves. We surfed until we were tired and hungry. Then we had a delicious seafood lunch. After lunch, I walked along the beach to collect some rina/shells. I found some special rina to take home for my sons.

Knowledge Books and Software

15

Day 5 was sunny with crystal clear water. It was time for another surf! Sometimes I paint my surfboards with Aboriginal art. This board shows people sitting on the sand dunes along the beach. We share our beaches with many different animals. It's important to care for our beaches and the animals that live there.

Knowledge Books and Software

On Day 6, we went to a blowhole and watched the seals playing on the rocky islands. Long ago in lutruwita, nearly all the seals were killed by the seal hunters. The seal skins were used to make boots and clothes. Seals are now protected and their numbers are growing.

Knowledge Books and Software

19

On our last day in our camper van, we went fishing. If you are a First Nations person, you can catch fish with a fishing rod, a spear, or a net. First Nations people have fished in these waters for thousands of years. We only catch and keep what we need. This way, there is always some left for next time.

Knowledge Books and Software

21

We dropped off our camper van and explored nipaluna on our last day. The big mountain that looks over nipaluna is called kunanyi/Mt Wellington. It often has snow in winter. After our day of sightseeing, we said goodbye to James and his family and flew home to Bundjalung Country. I gave the rina to my sons and told them all about my adventures. I can't wait to visit lutruwita again!

Knowledge Books and Software

23

Word bank

palawa kani <pah lah wah kah nee>/Tasmanian Aborigines speak

lutruwita <lu tru wee tah>/Tasmania

nipaluna <nee pah lu nah>/Hobart

purinina <pu ree nee nah>/Tasmanian Devil

tukana <tu kah nah>/Tasman Peninsula

rina <ree nah>/shell

kunanyi <ku nah nyee>/Mt Wellington

adventure

Wiradjuri

European

meat-eaters

endangered

protected

Knowledge Books and Software